The Joshua Poems

by

Carolyn Light Bell

© 2023 Carolyn Light Bell. All rights reserved.
This material may not be reproduced in any form, published,
reprinted, recorded, performed, broadcast,
rewritten or redistributed without
the explicit permission of Carolyn Light Bell.
All such actions are strictly prohibited by law.

Cover image of Joshua by Carolyn Light Bell
Cover design by Shay Culligan

ISBN: 978-1-63980-448-1

Kelsay Books
502 South 1040 East, A-119
American Fork, Utah 84003
Kelsaybooks.com

for Joshua

Acknowledgments

I am surrounded by angels. They let me hold onto their wings as they flutter by, rising and falling with the current. My darling Eddie is first. I cannot imagine life without him. We talk about our children, all three, Stephanie, Randy and Joshua, in the middle of the night and at breakfast. Our son-in-law, Howard; daughter-in-law, Erin; and our grandchildren, Samuel, Isaac, Eleanor and Eliah, are all supportive and loving.

We lost an important person, our youngest child, Joshua, on September 14, 2020, and we'll miss him forever.

To name a few special friends who helped me through these first two years, I risk overlooking many. I apologize.

Thank you to Joshua's many friends who loved him, whom he loved back. We are deeply indebted to Peter Aamoth who brought part of Joshua's final story to us. Alexandra, Aviva, and Joanna, you are truly forever friends. My list of walking buddies who were there when we first learned, who listen, ask questions, speak truths, must include the one who heard first: Sharon Bottorff, who took over for us to host our neighborhood "night out" gathering; Judy Tennebaum, who came to greet me for a walk but instead heard my incredible news; Barbara Lordi, who makes me laugh so hard we both double over; Meryll Page, ever faithful, with a clarion voice, great kindness, sturdy fearlessness. Other dear friends include Barbara Goldfarb who knew Joshua from the time he was born and checks on me regularly; Barbara Glaser, who speaks straight truth; Marilyn and Martin Lipschultz, and their lovely daughter Jessica, all of whom knew and loved Josh, and know very well how to listen; Gracie Rogers, who has truly shared this journey day or night. Sylvia Horwitz has been close by my side throughout. I am grateful to Diane Gerstler and Alison Hartman, both of whom are insightful and wise. Also Diane Pecoraro who sees the poetry in life. Lucy Bruntjen and Liz Weir, my sweet, kind artist and poet friends, support my work and helped me through my writing these difficult poems—I am deeply indebted to you. Nancy and Tom Gould affirm and inspire me to be and to say exactly what I mean. Lee Woolman generously agreed to read my work in its final stages and to offer his helpful insights and penetrating questions, all of which advanced my own understanding. My therapist, Mark, has been with me from the beginning of Joshua's end. I have learned so much from him. He listens to me about myself, about Josh, about life. I would be a wreck without him.

Survivors' Resources holds Thursday night meetings for those of us whose loved ones died by suicide. All of you who participate, especially Brenda Darval, Caryl Lewis and Valerie Scatena, demonstrate courage just by showing up. Toni Plante leads our group with humor and compassion.

I am especially grateful to Steve Kaplan, a dear friend, who generously offered his invaluable expertise to get this book into your hands.

I hope these poems speak to you in some way. They won't answer all your questions. You may find this subject too hard. We all suffer loss. Suicide is very dark, especially if it's your child. Some of my poems may strike a chord in you, resounding and comforting you. May the beauty and spirit of Joshua carry you forward as it carries me.

A few of these poems were published in journals no longer in print. Those I remember are:

Sing Heavenly Muse: "So Much for Detachment"
Milkweed Chronicle: "Family Camping Trip," "Building Sandcastles in Lindau, Germany"

Contents

I. No Longer

A Fine Welcome	17
At the Playground in September	18
Joshua, Age Two, and I	19
Spring Balloons	20
Blue Ribbon Boy	21
Building Sandcastles in Lindau, Germany	22
Family Camping Trip	24
So Much for Detachment	25
I've Never Written About the Joy	27
Son of the Commandment*	29
Letting Go of the Last Child	31

II. Prescience

A Recurring Dream	35
A Witch in the Walls	36
Cars and Trucks	37
When Did It Get to Be Too Late?	38
Wellness Check	40
Joshua Speaks, Unabridged: A Three-Part Rap*	42
The Proper Way	45
A Dream of Blood	46
His Color Caught the Light*	47
Some Strange Package	48

III. Step by Step

Deadly	51
Hearts Don't Break	52
Suicide: I. Markers	54
Suicide: II. Los Angeles	55

A Misbegotten Gift	57
Never Apologize	59
Cycles of Grief	60
No Greater Loss	61
So Many Never Agains	62
Tinsel	63
Promises, Promises	65
Catching up	66
You'll Never Be an Old Man, Josh	68
What Happens to a Soul	69

IV. Forced to Swim

For Joshua's Descendants	73
How Shall I Then Live	75
Did I Accompany Him?	77
Honor Winter	78
Things I'd Want to Know	79
Wild Bird	80
All Good People Die	84
Sometimes	85
Playing Mendelssohn on Joshua's Yahrzeit	86
No Thing Is Sacred	88
Spoons	89
Mourning	90
I Hear His Voice, I See His Hands	92
Living and Dying	93
Surrender	94
A Reflection	95
Finally	96

Preface

The truth is we lose our children the moment they are born. We trust they will be present at least until we ourselves leave the material world. I mourned the times I said goodbye to Joshua when he would go off to school, off to overnight camp, off to live on the West Coast. I dreaded the time we'd have to part. I'd come home and cry and wander in and out of his room, looking for him. On September 13, 2020, the day before he left us for good, he apologized first, told us he loved us. We hadn't heard from him in months, and he had hired an attorney to forbid us from getting in touch. After we talked, I told him I'd call him tomorrow, feeling so relieved he'd broken the silence, thinking we'd check in. We did not imagine he'd be gone on September 14.

These poems are about him. He rejoiced. He suffered. Both/and.

There are names and medical diagnoses that partly describe him according to current analyses, but they do not fully define him. He was described as having bipolar disorder and addiction, but he convinced us he was "fine" without the usual prescription medications. He tried talk therapy briefly, but said he was "under control." He used alternative methods of self-discovery, from marijuana to ayahuasca to kambo. They further confused his fragile brain chemistry.

Those who knew him thought he was one of the best people they'd ever known: compassionate, empathetic, funny, musical, brilliant, kind. All true.

Only a few people saw him in a full-blown manic episode. Thank you for your patient kindness.

These poems are also for you, the readers, for the ones who will cry and for those who can't. It's also for our entire family, all of whom are very, very brave, despite deep pain.

Someone asked me at a reading, "What should I say to you?"

Hold Joshua in your heart and mind, even if you didn't know him in person. Hold all those close who, like Joshua, find the world too painful to endure. Talk to those who are suffering. Secrets and pretense can be lethal. Never give up. Where there's life, there's hope. The empty space in my soul where Joshua lived will never be filled. Yet, I am immensely grateful the world gets fuller every day with loving people, rich and radiant.

I. No Longer

A Fine Welcome

You squirm
fresh from my womb.
Masked men in green gloves
hold you fast.
Swollen, mashed, and worn
from the journey,
tendrils of rebellion
curl about your ears.
Startled from a long dream,
you squeeze your eyes shut.
Nurses bathe your tender skin.
I offer you milk,
warm your tender blue fingers
in my hand,
cradle your tiny limbs,
our time together too brief.

At the Playground in September

I sit curled on a park bench,
waiting and worried,
watching you three weave
through private
contests.

Crawling son,
cottonwood twig in your mouth
like an old stogie,
padding forward,
into the singing wind.

Middle child,
rough and tumble boy,
super space hero
wielding a circus sword—
Thwack-thwack!

Beautiful daughter,
hanging upside down
by your ankles
from the jungle gym,
reminding me of decades ago

when I dropped from a jungle gym
to the unforgiving ground—
I kept it secret forever,
having turned suddenly deaf and dumb.
No one could know my disgrace.

Pretending we're perfect
is a terrible mistake.
No sense mulling over old wounds.
Three becomes four
in games I adore.

Joshua, Age Two, and I

Little son
in dark green overalls
and a gingham shirt
wipes tears from his cheeks
with the back of his fist.
I reach down to pick him up,
to comfort him,
and he strokes my hair.
Our cheeks stick fast
with salt and grief.
There is no apparent
reason to cry.
I know
I'll remember
this day forever
when he looked so sweet
but turned
in con sol able.
He and I
held mirrors up
to our own inexplicable secret.

Spring Balloons

His bright pink balloon,
with a curling green string,
holds promise, like spring flowers.

He flies with it,
feet skimming earth,
flicks his wrist and grins.

Our small son wants it to fly,
so he lets it go up to the sky,
and I cry, "No!"

Chasing the bobbing string,
trees take him
out of sight.

My memory fills to bursting
and pops swift as a dream.
Our small son is grown and gone.

He studies the art of film
and other dreams, soaring
in and out of sight.

Outside there is sleet.
Much of the world lies still.
Another friend is dying.

My husband stands under the skylight,
says he'll kiss me once before he shaves
and once afterwards.

He's bright as the brightest balloon,
and I'm afloat in a sky
filled with floating balloons.

Blue Ribbon Boy

On your fifth birthday
you run to breakfast
like a colt,
all legs.
Clumps of mane
stick up
wild and shiny.
In your eyes
is the race ahead;
in my hands,
applause.

Building Sandcastles in Lindau, Germany

I.

On the shores of the Boden See
we built a rock wall
to keep out enemy.
Shaped, it was a castle.
A careful garden grew
with sticks and reeds
of landscape, an oasis
where castlefolk could
meditate. It then became
a fish: medieval castlefish
with wildflowers.
Satisfied, we'd live there.

II.

The next day
imitations had sprung up,
crude and clumsy likenesses.
We were surrounded
by suburban sprawl.
A nude baby stood sandy-assed
within our borders,
sucking on a stone.
We weren't flattered.
Nor did we squat all day
to watch developments.

III.

It was plain that once we made
our castle public, it was
no longer ours. It evolved into a style,
then precursor. We were powerless.
but our joy had been in its creation.
The gift coursed through our hands.
In time, water breaks down—
wildflowers, rock, castle, style,
gift, hands, baby.
Resistance is just a stage.
What remains is simple
flow of water over sand.

Family Camping Trip

Homebound
on either side of the freeway,
cars strain with the load
of boats and trailers.
Some are tiny home replicas,
complete with welcome mats.

After a month, our Vanagon reeks
of rotting meat and dirty clothes.
Three brown bodies, swollen
with bites, snooze and sprawl.
One, on the floor, mouth open,
shorts pulled tightly up
around his genitals, shares
his space with the dog,
a jug of water, assorted maps.

On the rear deck, the smallest
scratches his patchwork face
of scabs. The eldest wakes
in front, turns on disco tunes.
Father scowls behind the wheel.
When we get home, we'll no longer
hunt the loon's egg
or smell a bonfire.

We'll put our milky glasses
in the dishwasher, call
our friends and sort mail.
Mayfly shells cling to our camper
screen, their fragile frameworks
a sign that each action taken,
no matter how random or dark,
is a transpiration of light,
a breath.

So Much for Detachment

I haven't always been there for you.
Other mothers sprang from sidewalks
just in time to right an almost fallen
bike or serve as Solomon
in squabbles over toys.

Once a crowd of neighbors had to saw
your spokes apart to free your foot.
When I arrived, they hovered round
like hired mourners, tsking tongues.

But this time I was right behind you
when you fell, a blur and then a small
blue heap—motionless, eyes slammed shut,
blood raisins in your nose.
I couldn't get my skis off fast enough.

Wake, little one. Wake up.
Don't let the snow god get you.
*What? Me call the ski patrol? I have to stay
here pressed to the icy ground,
watching you breathe. Here they come—
three stooges in slow brown clownsuits
and yellow crosses, arguing technique
of rescue. Hell, I can move faster than that!*

Your eyes fluttered, fixed on me. We bumped
down slopes, coarse blanket flapping
on your face, a shroud.
Doctors fought like fools to claim you.
Now you lie with broken thumbs
and a concussion, hooked to monitors.
I pause at each quick breath, my own pulse
riding the rise and fall of your sheets.

You dream of trees and jungle damp
swinging from limb to limb, you wrap
your thumbs round vines in perfect brachiation
while I sit frozen in the shadows, rooted
to your white bed.

Your healing will be faster than mine.

I've Never Written About the Joy

I've never written about
the absolute joy of each one's birth—
Stephanie born on an April day
when I wore ribbons in my hair,
Randy born on a bright May day
after the arc of a scarlet sunrise,
Joshua born last to surprise me
when I expected a girl.

I've never written about the joy,
spying Joshua in the field of four-year-old faces
at four fifteen, after a long day of teaching.
At last! Full of aching guilt, I'd cry
when he leapt into my arms and we,
both anxious to hug and sniff and kiss,
drove home to the swaying, black fluff
of a dog whose tail beat a solid rhythm against our legs.

I've never written about the joy
when after days of planning and cleaning
for my daughter's twelfth birthday,
she smiled and said, "Oh, Mommy!"
in a grownup voice, standing on a stool
to peek into the floral bag
and then, unable to resist, tore open the paper
of a bouquet of white flowers, all for her.

I've never written about the joy
as I watched them all
finally not fighting over
who got the extra cookie,
but instead constructing
Lego spaceships, castles and cars
all three children together,
quietly, on the orange shag rug.

I've never written about the joy
when I heard "Thank you,"
or "You're a good cook," or "You're nice."
When they asked questions like "Is God in walls?"
or "Will you play with me, Mommy?"
When one night our whole family madly rode bikes
around Lake of the Isles, competing to see who could go
farthest no-handed and were bombarded by bats.

I've never written about
the joy of caring for their needs
with Band-aids, long lectures
and new clothes.
I've never written about
the joy of having both boys and a girl—
the thrill of watching small bodies grow.

I've never written about the joy of reading
stories at night while rocking them,
tucking in their sleepy selves
tiptoeing past their curled shapes
to turn out the light,
certain I'd see them again in the morning,
all fuzzy with hair sticking out
and stale breath, wanting breakfast.

I've never written about
the joy of learning
each other's inconsistencies
and tantrums, rantings and whims,
and at the end of the day
be all kisses and hugs
adoring each other anyway
because—well, just because.

Son of the Commandment*

Bright child of joy
you mend the broken,
warm the cold
bring light to darkness.

Born right after your father's birthday
and two days before mine,
you are the binding gift
of our love
as third in this family,
but not the last
in families to come.

Bubbling boy
full of dreams for the world
you stretch across days
with your lengthening legs
striding into the future
smiling, dimples and braces gleaming,
white Phantom guitar slung at your hip
strumming Stairway to Heaven.

Assemble yourself
for the world is wondrous
as a clear night sky full of stars
more awesome than X-Men
as rich a blend as October's reds
over Cedar and Balsam Lake
even greater than your best
waterski rooster tail
but bittersweet
like black chocolate.
May you savor it all.

Remember your name, Joshua,
and fit every battle in Jericho.
Lead, Abraham,
after your great grandfathers
Abraham Light and Abraham Wallach,
your great grandmothers Lena and Minnie
after your grandfathers
Randolph Light and Samuel Bell
your grandmothers
Mildred Lohmann and Ethel Bell
after your parents
and before your grandsons
and granddaughters
whatever their names will be . . .
Lead in peace.
Go forth and begin.

* I read this on the bimah at Joshua's Bar Mitzvah

Letting Go of the Last Child

We circled round the issue
until with gentle brutality
you tell me to stop grilling you,
that you're old enough now—

old enough to stop answering questions
about your whereabouts,
how much you had to drink,
who was at the party.

Old enough to slip into our room
after dark and say goodnight
without my knowing or caring
about the time.

Old enough to lean down to embrace
my stiffening body and soul
to drive to your lessons,
auditions, and ski meets.

But am I old enough, youngest child
to let you go, finally, to stop
wanting to kiss your dimpled cheeks,
to tell you the truth about life?

Will I ever stop this longing
to reach into your childhood again,
to stop time, to keep you from
driving away, without driving you away?

II. Prescience

A Recurring Dream

All through your childhood
I dreamed of you
falling through the cold metal rungs
of a jungle gym.
I would look up
from below
as you came down
toward me
falling.
I would watch you
fall
helpless
to catch you.

You were such a
precious child
too good
to be true,
spinning and twirling
fast and furious
like maple seeds
in autumn wind.
I grew dizzy
as I watched you
fall
through the rungs
of your life.

A Witch in the Walls

When you were young
you saw a witch in the walls.
You cried when she appeared
and begged me to make her
go away.

I explained to you
that she was in your mind,
that there was no witch.
But you were unconvinced.
I found a cougar poster.

I propped the cougar
next to the window by your bed,
ready to pounce at your command.
It helped you to know
the power of mind.

In later years
I reminded you
of the cougar and the witch,
and you reminded me
the witch was real.

Cars and Trucks

"What kind of sheets do you want for college?"
"I don't know, Mom.
Let's go look at some."
He picked out Cars and Trucks.

"Really?" I said.
Joshua held fast to childhood,
the boy who claimed he wasn't sentimental.
Sweet, sweet child.

I kept his cars and trucks sheets
for twenty-five years
and with misgivings handed them
to the cleaning lady

who tore them up
and folded them into a plastic tub
to use for rags
to wipe clean the dust.

We have no more Josh
except a small hand-carved
box of ash, the remainder of life
now driven away.

And now I want his sheets—
the bright red car,
the fat yellow truck,
the happy blue dots.

I want him back.
his smile, his face,
his heart,
his lovely, lovely soul.

When Did It Get to Be Too Late?

to turn back
to return to the wholeness
of you
when you were young—
the   not
broken   ness?

Did we try hard enough
to help you fill
the fissures in your brain
where bewitching
deviant chemicals
stupefied you,
intensified your confusion
and swelled to a tsunami?

The poisonous pandemic
and a frightened wife
seized your innocent child
and fled, leaving you alone,
ferocious fears
torturing your soul
with lightning flashes
that surged and finally
struck you still?

Your resistance was,
in the end, too feeble.
Your mind,
distended with delusion,
choked out
every molecule of fresh air.
Every memory of love and hope
flattened to despair.

You will never be whole.
You will never be young
or old.
You gave up hope, dear son,
but we, on a fool's errand,
could not. We tried from home.
We sent the cops.
Our failure will never be right
and in the end there is no wrong.

Wellness Check

The cops kept coming
creeping quietly to your curb
so as not to be seen.
When they knocked, you opened
the door and said, "What do you want?
There's no problem here!"

And they found you alive
and you said you were fine
and they believed
and so they left.
And they kept coming
because we kept sending them.

"Are you a danger
to yourself or others?"
Yes, you were, although you lied again,
saying "no" because you couldn't admit the truth
and the cops kept coming
and they finally cuffed you.

Your fear was confirmed.
They caught up with you.
Your chemistry askew.
Your belongings astrew.
Your neighbors on cue
took pictures. We knew:

You'd lost control at last.
Your mind had crashed.
Your house was trashed.
Your marriage was past.
All hopes were dashed.

They took you in
for the seventy-two—
but it wasn't enough.
It was never enough.
You needed much more than that,
much, much more than that.

No cop could bring you wellness
and neither could we,
however we tried
and in the end you created
your suicide rap.

Joshua Speaks, Unabridged: A Three-Part Rap*

I. Far from Home

To live and die in LA, in pursuit of my dreams . . .
Just forget about it. Just go back to your life . . .
Suicide's an overdose, mental murder;
my punishment's deserved.
Hazardous like Lazarus with an asterisk.
Caught between two worlds . . . pain around it
Shame around it
Getting sick with new girls
calling me Daddy, pulling on my curls.
The rest I made up off my tippy-toppy.
Call me Rabby-jabby.
It's so easy to get breezy
nice and easy.
I paint a picture like the Mona Lisa
with a half-smile, like my freestyle.
Can you feel it?
Nothing can save you.
I'm peeling myself off the ceiling,
I'm reeling back. Younger days I will attack.
Hop, skip, and jump away to the moon.
I consume the image.
I used to travel around on my bicycle.
I added a wheel and now it's a tricycle
Drop two it's a unicycle.
I learned to balance with a strong core.
I explore

---

* Randy, Joshua's brother, downloaded Joshua's entire hard drive onto an external drive, from which I transcribed these three final raps, all in his own words. Joshua filmed himself, rapping with a percussive background, in his home studio. His microphone lit up with tiny lights, he filmed increasingly finished versions on different days, wearing various outfits, reading the words out of his journal, until he was satisfied. For the last one, "Sick of it All," he sat on a tall pile of clothes with various instruments placed within camera range.

like Magellan, an ill rap felon,*
eating watermelon, spitting out the seeds.
I shall proceed to give you what you need,
spreading my seed around the land.
I disseminate, I elevate now.
I lay back and meditate.

I conversate:
I paint a picture for you.
I think that you deserve it.
I'm here to serve it.
Smack it and flip it and rub it down—
that's my sound.
I'm having fun with my lyrical dun.
I'm far from home—
a hundred miles of runnin'.
I never stopped
living in an Upside Down World.

II. AND I AND I AND I

I do the Body.
I do the Cabbage Patch.
I do Mr. Sprinkler, Mr. Sprinkler.
It's just me, myself and I
and I and I and I
get so high.
I wonder why
I'm flyin' with the cosmonauts.
I say "What's Up?" to Boris Yeltsin.
I do the whatnot.
You catch me laughin'

---

* In hip-hop jargon, ill means *crazy good*. Hence, an ill rap felon (e.g. Magellan) was crazy good at what he did (explore).

cruisin' by your giraffin'.
"What's Up?" to Mr. Hippopotamus,
my hippothalmus,
my hippocampus,
pulling ladies off the campus.
Dangerous for your health
I pull books off the shelf
living in an upside-down world.

wondering if you can hear me now,
asking you to heal me now.
Living underneath it all.
Wishing I was ten feet tall.
Loving you is all I know.
Giving you this love I grow.
Wishing I was with you now.
Loving you can heal me now.

III. Sick of It All

Sick of it all.
Just sick and tired of it.
Sick of you, sick of me,
I want none of it.
It's not that I'm runnin',
I've just run out of words.
I'm just so m.f. sick of it all.
You won't respect my time-outs.
My thoughts get disturbed.
I'm a stranger in a strange land.
I was broken from birth,
just barely from this earth.
This is not an apology.
My cocoon's built for one.
Baby, I'm so sorry, but now I gotta run.

The Proper Way

We held him briefly on our laps,
smelled the sweetness of his breath.
Soon he grew to be a man.
With a swift glance
over his broadening shoulder
he gave a wave as brave as his smile.

Step by step
he left us
in his wake,
the way folks say
is The Proper Way
all children must leave.

Had we truly known
how improper he truly was
how out of balance
how buckled, how bent
how unfixed
beneath the face of perfection . . .

It was Not
The
Proper
Way
at all—
not   at   all.

A Dream of Blood

I'm trying to do everything right
but I am hemorrhaging.
Stephanie is with me.
I am huddled up against a wall.
There is so much blood.
I try to clean it up
but every time I lean over,
there is more.
A Native woman in a line of women
says, "Oh, look! She lost her baby!"
I have lost Joshua.
Huge clots of blood.
I lost my baby. My baby.
Beautiful golden baby turned to blood.

His Color Caught the Light*

and split into rainbows.
He grew the tallest of three—
adored and envied,
a prize
gifted beyond measure.

Spilling with talent
yet secretly unsure—
full of mystery,
humor,
and abiding love.

* I wrote this poem the day after Josh died, and sent it with photographs of him surfing (see cover), on memorial cards to be sent to the hundreds of people who sent notes after he died.

Some Strange Package

My old therapist called
after Joshua died,
"I'm sorry," she said.
Yes.
There it is.
Bipolar disorder. Addiction. Suicide.
I had nothing more to say.
Like some strange package
thrown at our door
neither of us wanted
to pick up or describe.
It had come true. It was real.
The nightmare of nightmares.

What can anyone say?
There are no right words.
Don't speak or ask,
"Whatever happened?"
Mystery transcends knowledge.
Yet she picked it up to examine its contents . . .
"It's not your fault."
What made you think I would think it was?

We could call it
an accident of the mind,
a misstep, a wrong assumption.
Inevitable.
A dark serpent descends,
an ouroboros
that devours its own tail
and disappears into eternity.

III. Step by Step

Deadly

How are you?
What's going on?
How've you been?
What have you been doing?
How's your writing?
Anything new?

They aim
right between
my eyes—
rat-a-tat, tat-a-rat!
Not pausing to reload
or mark my response.

Their questions
are assault rifles
peppering me with questions
piercing my skin
leaving holes in my heart
no breath between.
Fully automatic.

Hearts Don't Break

Born with few boundaries,
he bounded over middle ground.
His lens captured raw brutal reality,
jagged edges,
the distress of extreme closeup.
Sought after as filmmaker,
a hungry fire burned
beneath his tender soul.
He strained to document burning fields
disarrayed with spinning spheres
and insatiable dreams.

Traveling solo
on a treacherous journey,
teeth clenched, jaw grinding, spirit dying,
he drove down the darkest spiral of unknowing.
In bold black marker,
up his forearm and hand,
he wrote, "I am a warrior.
I am a healer. My soul will never die."

Unable to wait any longer,
or endure the loneliness
or disguise the pain
or stop the suffering
or mend the broken,
he leapt o'er a ruined world,
losing the battle he tried
so hard to win.

Left behind, spilling from the doors of his home
were a dozen stage microphones,
camera bodies and lenses in multiple sizes,
thousands of vinyl records,
amplifiers and turntables,
surfboards and bicycles,
hats and suits and shirts,
like unruly soldiers, lined up and
sold in a few days on-line,
by a slick alchemist-auctioneer named Phil,
whom Joshua's ex-wife hired to line her pockets,
melting Joshua's treasures into cash.
Hearts don't break,
they stop beating.
Hearts don't break,
people do.

All that we love we lose.

Suicide: I. Markers

The subject terrifies.
Don't wince.
Learn it.
Markers exist.
Male gender. Check.
Living alone. Check.
Caucasian. Check.
Suicide ideation. Check.
Previous Hospitalization. Check.
Rapid cycling subtype. Check.
Which came first, the drugs
or the disorder?
The concussions or the
disease?
The chicken or the egg?
Encephalopathy?
Were you marked from birth
and we didn't recognize it?
We thought what we saw
was just Josh.

Suicide: II. Los Angeles

How could you?
Your father sadly said, "He had it all."
Here's how: LA is what you sought,
with plastic-lined streets
sheer and fragile
cluttered with chaos
and unfettered phoniness
where the depths of your soul
wanted to believe
in the stick-thin skin
of zombie-walkers called men
and women dealing toxins
like marijuana,
ayahuasca and frog venom.
Your laughter once real
became false facing odds
insurmountable
the terrible odds of surviving
honesty intact or balls
borne, bred and bouncing
with the fine crazy-real
reel of the Midwest.
You shipped off your sanity
to wander unknown shores
of too-hot sun and too many cars.
Tinsel town was all shiny;
you fit in transmogrified
transformed into madness
wanting it all, wanting it all—
your house in Atwater
your women in-house
your job as director
and every techno toy
you could buy on-line.

Life couldn't hold you
like that. You blew up,
just plain wore yourself out
and we are left dazed,
deceived by your green screen
standing, staring
at a star   dust
trail   that   was   you.

A Misbegotten Gift

She'd like to pretend he never existed,
rewriting the script of their life,
concocting a fabulous lie,
alleging a hundred plus pages of hateful hokum
sent to her attorney, to ours, and then to me
because we wanted to visit Bowie,
Joshua's child, our granddaughter.
We wanted to keep loving Bowie
like we keep loving Josh.
But with razor-sharp intent
and blunt confabulation,
she severed connection to all ten
of Joshua's immediate family members.
A misbegotten gift to our granddaughter
is her excision of my family name and Joshua's last name,
keeping only Bowie's first name, adding two madcap names.

I'm here to lay claim to the fact
of Joshua's existence, his fatherness,
his fallibility. His daughter will always be his
and ours. No one can erase genetics.
or wipe out his good name.
I'm here to say he was wonderful
and she is cruel.
I'm here to say she can never wipe out his life.
Only he had the power to die by suicide
and to live on in our memories as kind and sensitive
a soul who happened to be very ill.
And she, wearing spangled boots and a sparkling smile,
watched from a distance
as he clung, alone,
to the sharp edge of a steep cliff.

And she, without mercy,
paid attorneys
to stomp on his fingers
until, unable to hold on,
he finally fell, desperate and dying,
to the very real earth.

Never Apologize

Don't cover your face
when you're cryin'.
Who shamed us to fear
our most natural feelings?
Instead of shunning, embrace.

Sadness and gladness,
laughter 'n tears,
spring hard and spring soft,
welling up from the same source
God gave us to feel.

Dalai Lama in saffron, "Arch" Tutu in pink
stroked arms as old pals unabashed.
First giggling, next weeping,
like babies, like old men.
No one said to them, "Stop!"

Honest love hides
neither sun rays nor rain.
So neither should you. No,
neither should you. For the natural music
of laughter or tears? Apologize? Never!

Cycles of Grief

Tonight I'm an empty gourd,
seeds scooped out long ago
and dumped in a pit
with other vanities of human endeavor.
My veins are but yellow strings
left clinging to the floor of their source.
Stripped and scraped until dry,
my flesh now lined and loose.
I've been left out in the storms,
depleted by this season of grief.

Sadness rolls in and rolls out—
unpredictable, irregular.
Summer's bounty has dwindled.
It's late in the year.
My harvest is over.
Time for spring fruit.
I relinquish my role as Demeter,
replaced by what's fresh,
one filled with new dreams.
Persephone awakes.

No Greater Loss

Eddie shows me a shredded glove,
leather freshly chewed to strips
and tossed around
by our two rambunctious pups.
I barely glance at it
before I plunge it deep in the trash.
I'll wear the one that's left.
They were old.
It doesn't matter.
What could matter
after the greatest loss
we've ever known?

So Many Never Agains

Never again will he surprise me on my birthday
hiding behind Eddie's study door.
Never again will he coach Bowie in "A Tisket, a Tasket."
Never again will he pop her into the swing
he hung from the lanai—
she, squealing with excitement, pink rubber boot
straps flapping to the rhythm of her feet.
Never again will he demonstrate to her
how to kick a soccer ball.
Never again will he be the gracious recipient
of my snapshots, be it a blazing red maple
or a dew-laden rose.
Never again will he suffer in silence.
Never again will he disarm a room with his charisma.
Never again will he listen to my tales of woe
and render wise counsel much cherished.
Never again will Bowie say, "My daddy is a film director,"
but rather, "My daddy was a film director."
Never again will I listen to his laughter.
Never again will I hear the furnace clanging
or smell skunks mating in our California February.
Never again will Bowie knock softly on our door
wanting oatmeal and blueberries for breakfast.
Never again will he shine
starlight on me,
my path brightened
by his too-brief life.

Tinsel

From across the room,
my father and I tossed tinsel
toward the Christmas tree,
hoping some would land
on the branches' green tips.
A few shiny, silver strands draped
and decorated the branches.
Most fell to the carpet beneath.

Like tinsel, genetic traits fall into place
along a twisted ladder that we climb,
beautiful and delicate as white pine.
No one knows what to expect,
when we straighten our knees down and then up,
playing a portentous game
of Ouija.

We count the good genes, ignoring the bad.
Our eldest, Stephanie, gives generously like her dad,
watches birds and words like me.
Our middle, Randy, straightens to exactitude
and speaks with rapier wit like my dad.
Our youngest, Josh, loved jazz and blues like me,
beamed a kind and gentle smile like Eddie.

Though he didn't let on he was unsafe
climbing his ladder of genes
without support, we held the rails,
hoping and holding.
We gaped up as he rocked back and forth,
tipping the balance.
Our hands quavered.
How could he reach such unreachable heights.

Fogged by altitude
not meant for mortal souls,
he let go. Off the ladder he flew.
Down and down he tumbled,
landing hard and forever.
We who had witnessed his ascent
now watched his fall, holding on
to his image streaming flat and bright.

Promises, Promises

People promise, "Memories will bring back the joy."
Really? Have you heard the sound of sobbing?
Have you seen the dull stare of sadness?
Have you felt the fall into a dark abyss?
Have you smelled the dank?

What can I do about Joshua's child, Bowie?
Her mother stole her from us. What of her?
A solid limb ripped wrongly from our family's tree.
"She'll seek you out when she's of age."
No kidding? I'll be dead.

"He's at peace," people say.
At peace?
I hold his little round box of ashes
in my palm and take a taste.
This is peace? Ash?

Catching up

"I'd like to catch up," says one,
not meeting my eyes.
"Let's catch up," says another,
raising her car window.

I am not a New Year's card
here to report the events of last year.
This was a lifetime rift
but maybe you can't understand.

What does catching up mean?
You want a summary
and all I can do is describe
one more fleeting moment:

a fritillary alight on the fringe of a bee balm
a cottonwood's whisper in the wind
a vision of Joshua to mist my eyes
or shake my shoulders.

I am keening with a sound new to me—
somewhere between wailing and shrieking
Please do not apologize for your words
just because they don't match mine.

In my world, there is a deep well
that connects to the core of the earth.
It doesn't fill up or spill over.
It circles and sucks.

It has its own tide.
Tide repeats itself
backward and forward again,
sometimes fierce, sometimes calm.

Tide is never at rest
or at peace. There is no peace.
I don't believe in peace
or in catching up.

One wave pulls up behind another
and a new one stretches up
o'ertaking the one in front.
But it never catches up.

There is no catching up—
only the continuous flow
of life without him,
and I am drowning in death.

You'll Never Be an Old Man, Josh

You'll never be an old man, Josh.
You'll always be a tall,
and engaging young man,
someone people turn their heads to see
with stunning good looks
and a confident walk
despite pronating ankles
and pigeon toes.

You won't have the pain
of stooped shoulders
and gravelly voice
eyebrows unruly
and stubbly chin,
musing over mischief
and dancing down stories
half conjured by mystical you.

You'll never be an old man, Josh.
You'll always be elegant,
stylish and trim,
arms still strong
and gait straight ahead.
I wish you could be here
to see Bowie grow tall,
to feel her embrace and those of her child,
filling the rest of your life with love.

What Happens to a Soul

If I met Joshua again,
would his energy be fiery,
his brilliant brain
overheating?

Or would he be gentle
sweet starlight,
beaming warmly
as a distant dream?

Would he return
to his origin—
laughing without mania,
crying without remorse?

Would he be afloat in air,
released at last
like his pink balloon,
out of sight but not mind?

I hope he'd be shining
with the pure face of God.
Isn't this, at last,
what happens to a soul?

IV. Forced to Swim

For Joshua's Descendants

Follow the unknown path.
Every living thing teaches,
Don't worry if you run
when you could walk,
or walk when you could run,
or if you mix up head and heart,
eye and hand.

Remember you're part fish
breathing through gills
you forgot you once had.
Dive to depths unplumbed.
Rise up when ready,
breaking through surface.
Inhale, renewed.
Plunge again.

You're also part heron
wading in shallows—soundless,
stroking water with stalky legs.
Strike when it's right, broadening wing.
Fish in beak, lift into a far-off wind,
feet unfettered,
earning grace.

Salvage what shines
on abandoned shores:
algae, gems, and stardust.
Weave it all through
your bleached-out dreamcoat
with threads of hope
beyond water and land.

Stitch together a crazy comforter
of fins and feathers,
unfinished journeys,
selves and souls that weakened,
split apart and fell to earth.
Wrap yourself in glory. Build a raft
that floats on a river of ancestral tears.

You, his beautiful nephews, niece and daughter,
Learn the opalescent beauty of all substance.
Celebrate the tensile strength of sorrow.
Wind streaming garlands
Through your hair.
Grief and joy are borne one.
For Joshua's sake, breathe.
Swim home.

How Shall I Then Live

Without him
Without his call at 9 pm
when we were asleep:
"Hi, Mom!"
Without his ringtone
driving home from taping
at Minnesota Radio Talking Book
"Crickets!! It's you!!"
Without texting my latest photographs:
a maple cluttered with autumnal leaves
blood-splotched and persimmon;
a split-rail fence sculpted in snow.
"Nice!" he'd say.
Without our winter's drive to LA,
pulling up
his standing at the curb smiling.
Without his rolling our suitcases
up the driveway
to our little house.
Without the feel of his embrace
when we said goodbye
and goodbye and goodbye.

With him
in a tiny hand-cut wood box
ashes strange and bitter
like nothing else
I've ever tasted.
With the beads he wore
whose origin remains unknown
and I wear hanging from my neck
when I need him close.
With my nighttime dreams
of his triumphs:

"I'm Captain of the World!"
With how he mastered the kitchen
in boxer shorts and sweatshirt
holding a freshly brewed mug of espresso.
Sometimes smiling,
sometimes rushed.
Usually offering,
"Want some?

Did I Accompany Him?

If you count the days and nights
I stayed up before and after
he died, talking to him,
consoling, pleading—
Yes, I accompanied
him in my heart.

Yesterday, a friend's dog, Flora, died.
Flora, in her arms,
closed her eyes for the last time
and my friend wondered,
Where did Flora go?

I know it's the place
where all souls go,
the place we cannot fully know
until we go. When we're there
we finally truly know.

Meanwhile, we tuck them
inside the pockets of our souls,
beyond
the curves, the crevices
and crenellations

until each of us rises to exist eternally—
hidden microbes in an atmosphere
we cannot fathom until we become
the terrifying and magnificent rapture
held forever   in the Yes   of love.

Honor Winter

Turquoise sky turns slate.
Winter sets in.
Crystalline beauty
stalks my heart.
I, a child born
in autumn,
turn toward
lengthening night
with longing.

My breath
grows frost
on its edges.
Snowy landscape ices
over these long months.
I slide across each slick surface,
balancing
between fierce wind,
the fire within.

Soon enough,
cardinals trail reeds
to rebuild nests,
in spruce trees.
I watch in awe
at how natural it is
for them to relinquish
the past, instructing me
to turn toward spring.

Things I'd Want to Know

When you were little and you told me, "I dream the future,"
what did you dream?

What was it that kept you from showing us your sad heart?

Why did you think you had to do it all?

Where did you get the beads you wore that I now treasure?
What wonderful adventure were you on?

If you truly believed in accepting the frailties of others,
why couldn't you accept your own?

What more proof did you need to know that you truly were
extraordinary?

What were you most afraid of?

Why did you think you were abused?

Why did you push us away when you needed us most?

What do you most want for your beautiful daughter?

When you called and said, "I'll figure it out,"
did you know you would take your own life?

Could you have imagined how much we'd miss you?

Wild Bird

I'm almost home, walking 'round the lake.
Ahead of me, wheels scraping sidewalk,
a woman pushes a walker,
tugging at her sagging pants.

Slow, but steady, with a little skip-hop,
sparkly pockets on her blue jeans,
ecru hat, brass studs on the brim,
hair grey as mine, but curly and thick as rope.

We pause to assess. She turns her face up to me
and smiles as friend. Missing teeth,
she still has style—
glamorous old bird, fallen from sky.

"Hard for you to push a walker
when you're holdin' up your pants?"
Gauging my tone, she cracks,
"Yep. Sure is. See, I don't have a butt."

"Would'ja like a belt?" I ask. "Yes, I would," she trills.
Name's Kelly with a y. Last name's Rosen,
but I'm not Jewish. I'm native. Now, Black women?
They got butts and all. Natives don't have shit."

"Hold on. I'll get you a belt."
I race home and bring back three:
black patent, Mexican multicolor,
and a long purple linen sash.

I bring her belts, bottled water,
cut up apple and a birthday cupcake.
"Peanut butter okay?"
She takes it and smiles again.

Belts are a lost cause since she's
thin as a ruler. I take them all back
and pat a park bench. "Belts aren't gonna work.
Sit down here. Eat up. Be right back."

Hurrying now, afraid she'll fly away,
this hungry wild bird.
I hustle home, drop the belts,
sling suspenders over one shoulder, race back.

"How was the cupcake?" I ask.
"Delicious. You're a sweetie."
"Stand up now," I say, lifting her thin bones.
I'm on a mission, without a "please."

We struggle. I reach under her hooded shirts.
Together, we arrange and fasten
front and back.
The buckles hold.

We sit down on the bench, leveling.
I tell Kelly about Joshua.
"That's sad," she says,
"I lost my man three years ago."

Our stories lift in the air, become clouds.
Josh had a home but didn't stay.
Grounded, Kelly has no home
and walks all day.

She throws her head back,
drinks the last drop,
crushes the bottle, cupcake wrapper,
and napkin into my hand.

I couldn't help Joshua.
All I can offer Kelly is suspenders,
a few snacks. I listen longer,
want to offer more.

Cars speed past us,
dogs barking out of car windows.
"I want a buckskin dress, mittens,
a place of my own."

Kelly owns what she wears,
plus a white plastic bag
knotted to her walker,
and a fringed purse.

Sun breaks bright discs on the waves,
a thousand mirrors.
The two of us reflect, selecting memories
from our common language. October's cold.

We shift. Time to go
where home is.
I glance at Kelly's long curved nails,
handy as dewclaws.

I barely blink before she's stretched
her wings and flown away. I'm left
pondering the lightest load
for her slender frame . . .

which pair of gloves
would fit close and warm,
strong as quills.
I imagine her next visit.

If a wild bird lights on a spruce limb
in winter, and I decide to feed her,
believe in her, I'd have to be there daily.
Her return is unlikely.

She wouldn't stay long,
perching for a breath,
curling long nails round,
piercing branches of my heart.

All Good People Die

One by one they leave us.
fading like stars at dawn.
We remember where they were,
that certain space they filled
in a day's embrace.
We hear their laughter
but cannot feel
their arms around us.

When the morning awakens me
to the hole in the day,
the new way,
the old place he left . . .
my mind chases his escaping shadow.
I seek to honor him anew.

You, our youngest child, our son . . .
Were you just a dream I left on my pillow?
Or were you once someone I called mine?
I understand now I own nothing—
not my family, my home,
not my friends, not even myself.

You belong to the lilacs
that we, your family, stood in a circle
at Old Pines to plant—
substance whose perennial glory
will reappear as white and violet tips
in April springtime—bundling together,
fading off and dropping down to seed.

Sometimes

"I wish he were here," says his brother.
He would have cheered me up."
What would he have said? I ask.
"That I always land on my feet.
That it will get better."

"Sometimes I reach in the basket
where I keep his old tee shirts
and I just smell his smell," says his sister.

Sometimes I wrap his necklace around my neck.
His ashes taste less bitter now,
in the third year. I hope
they last the rest of my life.
I kiss his photograph on my dresser.

"I think of him all the time,"
says his father, choking on sobs.

It's an all-the-time thing.
It doesn't go away.
We don't move on.
We live with him
inside out. Day in. Day out.
At night when we least want to.
In public when it surprises us.
Some   times   truly   is
All   The   Time.

Playing Mendelssohn on Joshua's Yahrzeit

I wrap myself in the memory
of him, the music of him
the *reverie*
the *consolation*
the *confidence*
all *songs without words.*

As if now, he is bringing Bowie in his arms
to the side of the piano, setting her
down beside me on the bench as I play.
Sunday, at his commemoration,
people spoke of how
he took his music with him wherever he went.
He had to have it.

When we ate dinner together,
he played jazz and rhythmic harmony
for the five of us—Joshua, his wife,
Bowie, Eddie and I—
gritty meals and jazzy sounds—
misty notes in air.

All his records were sold at auction,
all his vinyl—
millions of sounds
now notes in the wind.
I let them go without a whimper.

"He had a soul," Eleanor said.
His soul wraps around us,
drifting in the moisture of my breath,
on my fingers as I play.

I see him coming again and again
to listen to me playing Mendelssohn,
Bowie in his arms.
"Listen! G. Mommy's playing the piano."

Now I try to play Mendelssohn but can't.
I restart with Bronislau Kaper's
Hi Lily, Hi Lily, Hi Lo
"A song of love is a sad song,"
and I cry and cry
and then I move back to Mendelssohn
so I can really picture Joshua standing
next to me that day, smiling,
when he gently placed Bowie beside me,
the child he taught to sing *A Tisket, A Tasket,*
the girl I longed to teach to tap dance,
the girl I hope someday will follow her father
who loved music, who was music.

No Thing Is Sacred

We had some of his things
shipped from California—
from his home—
his coffee table I used to oil,
large and heavy,
made of mahogany or maybe cocobolo,
fashioned by his precious hands
with hairpin legs, and irregular edge,
in the rough shape of Minnesota;
his tiny spoons, impractical and strange;
a beige wool blanket he bought
at a Pendleton outlet when we were together.

Our friends admire these things,
as they should, at Old Pines,
our cabin he once called "magical,"
a place he visited and loved,
a place he'll never see again.
I eye each item closely,
terrified of further loss—
a spoon disappeared,
a blanket frayed, the table scratched.
No thing is truly sacred anymore—
It never really was—
except his memory.

Spoons

Four hungry teenagers—
Joshua's nephews and niece—
in haste and hunger have thrown together lunch at the cabin.
From the cupboard and fridge, we all pull canned lentil soup,
cheese, crackers, lemonade and cookies.
From the silverware drawer
they select tiny sherbet spoons whose bowls
are a deep, rounded shape.
Once seated, they try to slurp soup into their mouths
but soon begin to laugh. Soup dribbles down their chins.
"I know it's hard to use them," I say,
"They were Joshua's, so I like looking at them."
I remove the rest of these small spoons from the drawer
and line them up in tight formation,
their bowls nestled together, balanced on their sides,
close and intimate as family,
spooning.
"I think Josh admired the shape of them. They were part
of a set in his California home," I explain.
"Did he use them?" asks Isaac, one of Joshua's nephews.
"I don't know. Maybe to stir his coffee.
Maybe he knew they didn't work
but kept them anyway," I say,
looking away.
There is a long silence no one dares break.
Eleanor's eyes are brimming with tears.
"We'll never know," says Eliah, grinning,
head cocked, voice deep as a man's.
At seventeen, he accepts the mystery.
At almost eighty, I do not.

Mourning

—for Eddie

I saw you crying quietly
among the chattering guests.
I saw you neither eat a crumb
nor want to rest.

I heard the sobbing, throbbing
in your voice,
your plaintive word,
your upraised eye.

We live where perfect snow
is plowed in hours,
salt and sand strewn harshly down
to cover nature's frozen show.

Were we but ploughs
that cleared a path and drove on through
lest our narrow path not find its way?
Were we left without a clue?

It's over soon for those of us
who hurry through the day
and miss the sun in its descent.
Did we miss him that way?

I've seen our planet sold for lack of love.
I feel the grief in me arise, take hold.
Each season's short. Each risk is great.
We can't predict our children's fate.

I listen for the Tundra Swan in spring
whose call is high above and scarcely seen,
who quickly passes by, but carries hope
across the heavens, upon each wing.

Life's quick like that. At last we really know,
it's up to us to recognize the flit and sway
along the latticework of every day…
It's us, our life—so short! And then away.

I Hear His Voice, I See His Hands

I hear his voice
as I pore over photographs
and hear him, urging me.
"Stop! Forget all that, Mom. It's past.
Go on with your life."
That was his mantra. "Go on."
Yet, he could not go on.

I see his hands, full of hope and love,
documenting his terrace plantings,
displaying labels as he snaps the photographs,
hands so like his father's.
Strong. Capable. Hard-working.
Clean. Nails clipped short.
Hands you'd hold if you needed support.

He admired beauty in all things.
On an airplane, he pressed his camera to the window,
to catch the spectacle that was Los Angeles:
millions of lights broken into spokes of urbanity,
dozens of photos exploding with light.

I was there the day a double rainbow split,
arcing in the sky over his house.
Our whole neighborhood came out,
gathering in the street, snapping the scene.
Remember the day, Josh?

I hear his voice. I see his hands.
Laughing, his hand pressing my shoulder.
"You need to go on, Mom."

Living and Dying

You're on a solo journey, like it or not.
On a lucky day you'll find someone who amuses you.
You hitch a ride on their sixteen-wheeler.
You share a word or two.

It's comforting in the dark, watching
telephone poles speed past, night warriors.
From the warmth of the cab you're fooled
into believing it will be like this forever.

Soon one of you changes direction.
Blame it on the rhythm of your breath.
You hop off and say your goodbyes cuz
s/he's going to a darker place. Call it death.

Everything hurts all over again.
You find another who matches the tone of your ring,
whose voice trembles or bursts into laughter
at exactly the same time, same thing.

One thing for sure: Nothing lasts.
You write and you read, searching for just the right
words, constellations to illuminate.
The lesson repeats: Carry your own light.

When your hands lose their grip,
and you lose track of your last race,
it's your soul that maps out the route
and your soul that marks your place.

.

Surrender

And again, we witness autumn's
browning leaves and grass.

A biologist said,
"Every heart has a certain number of beats."

We strive for completion,
as we clamor for a final spot.

I reaffirm that I own nothing,
neither flesh nor breath.

I've earned nothing but my own death
turning color in surrender.

A Reflection

From the murmur of our first sounds
to the musical chording of our last . . .
Human imagination can't possibly predict what may happen
as time commutes us from moment to moment—
We rise at midnight pondering the message
of the last dream that woke us from slumber,
which child, friend or stranger will demand the most humor on
Monday,
which memory do we bury in a small box and which do we frame.
We complete one more act of love to someone in need.
We slow our pace to meditate, striving to amend our mistakes.
Maintaining hope and courage, we move forward, step by step,
into the magnificent and terrifying knowledge of death
that tomorrow will be ours.

Finally

We all blow away in the wind
like milkweed fluff grown from seed.
We finally yield to the soil, soft as pears.

It calls for bravery.
It calls for tears.
It calls for strength.

Others bear witness,
their eyes full of love,
hearts and souls encircling.

We lift and carry one another
up into a wilderness
we have never known.

We merge
with everyone and everything
that has perished before us.

As long as our breath holds out,
let us embrace every moment
with grace.

About the Author

Carolyn Light Bell is a photographer, writer, and educator. Her work has appeared widely, but her former students who express gratitude for being a positive influence on their lives bring the deepest satisfaction. Published works include *Delivery,* a collection of poetry; *I Heard a Fish Cry,* a collection of short stories; *Love's Little Triumphs,* a collection of short stories; *Eleanor and the Little Turtle* and *Lala and Her Friends,* bilingual children's books. She is the Chief Editor of *Pieces of Work, 36 Sermons, Conversations, Stories and Mystical Musings,* by the late Rabbi Sim Glaser, and the Editor of *A Collection of Meditations.*

www.ingramcontent.com/pod-product-compliance
Lightning Source LLC
Chambersburg PA
CBHW070936160426
43193CB00011B/1708